# Desires Cause Climate Change

**Dedication:** To Susan and Cara

**Disclaimer:** This book is a work of faction — a seed is planted, nurtured, and flourishes. It is based on theory and it's about the role of insights plays in our lives.



Copyright © Mark Dalliston 2020
ISBN: 978-1-71687-346-1

# Contents

# Introduction

"Surely if living creatures saw the results of all their evil deeds, they would turn away from them in disgust. But selfhood blinds them, and they cling to their obnoxious desires. They crave pleasure for themselves and they cause pain to others; when death destroys their individuality, they find no peace; their thirst for existence abides and their selfhood reappears in new births. Thus they continue to move in the coil and can find no escape from the hell of their own making" - Gautama Buddha

Nobody is talking about the real cause of climate change. Our desires are to blame. With the real cause found, we have the opportunity to cure our desires. We still have the time to turn this ship around. When we enter the red zone, it may be too late.

The red zone will arrive when there will be approximately 10 billion people. Then there is little chance of preventing our tipping point towards disaster. It is projected that the human population will stall about 2100 but we will still be in the red zone and polluting at the higher rates.

Malcolm Gladwell viewed a tipping point as a social phenomena. Our tipping point is a causation of climate change that reaches a majority believing and acting on the belief that climate change is real. The majority is important because if we reach participation at this level, we can prevent desires steering us in the wrong direction.

The Mount Erebus crash provides an example of what we mean. There were three identified causes resulting in the crash. They were identified as a flight course error, a pilot judgement error and a phenomenon known as whiteout. If any of these three causes had been absent, the plane may not have crashed. In this scenario, there are a few rather than a single causation identified event. These causes may be viewed as risk factors.

Desires may be the root cause of climate change but there are multiple risk factors involved. Any three of these risk factors may collectively cause a tipping point. These risks included population, pollution and fossil fuels. We are the primary cause of all three factors and hence the survival of Homo Sapiens, and most other life on Earth. There are many risks involved but only on root cause; the risks are necessary but not sufficient conditions.

If you are serious about finding the root cause of climate change, then we need look no further than our wants. Our wants are the principle source of climate change. We are responsible for rising temperatures on Earth through our wants. Our wants for red meat, travel and non-sustainable food sources drive climate change.

Wants are also the cause of suffering in our lives. If you want to solve the primary source of anxiety in our lives, then curb your wants. A cessation of all wants is a way to cure all our suffering. So is drastically curbing our desires and taking sustainability seriously. The choice is between the cessation of desires, which some may find too aesthetic, and curbing our wants but introducing global sustainability.

Pollution is identified as a major cause of our changing weather. There are at least major causes of pollution: industry, farming and plastics. These four pollute our air, waterways and cause greenhouse gases. Less waste and better air quality would be a bonus to solving increasing temperatures. A dramatic decline in the cow population would help decrease greenhouse gas emissions.

Drastically increasing air quality through less industrial combustion of natural resources. The manufacturing industry affects the quality of the air through the release of large amounts of carbon monoxide, hydrocarbons and organic compounds into the air. The petroleum refineries release hydrocarbons and other chemicals that pollute the air. Refineries also cause land pollution. Other pollutants are not so obvious when it comes to greenhouse gases and pollution.

We all know about the level of smog due to the combustion of petroleum. We don't realise the extent of the pollution through planes, trains and automobiles. We recognise that the larger the mode of transport the more emissions. But would you suspect mining and farming as the major cause of air pollution through chemicals, dust and plundering of natural resources.

All of this introduction reinforces the point that less desires means a lower chance of people destroying the earth. This means if we want a permanent solution, there is no better way than reducing our desires. We can't wait until our population reaches 10 billion. The amount of danger to the atmosphere increases through our waste and this increases the greater the population.

## Addiction requires rehab

We are addicted to our desires. By always wanting a bigger TV, a larger house and a new car we create our own suffering; we live beyond our means. Economic growth is a good thing when it is slow; when greed consumes all to meet our growth targets then we come off the rails and create the conditions for recessions. Profitability depends on a greedy economy that is full of our desires; all to avoid the next big crash.

Our wants are predicated on our delusion that we get X, we will be happy. What happens when you get a new car? We are happy for a fortnight then that elation begins to die down. There is a lull in our feeling of joy until our next purchase. Greed is fueled by our willingness to go into debt to satiate our wants. Debt is a good thing as it fuels greed. Like any addiction, you have to want to be treated for your addictions.

Our addictions make us happy, temporarily. That is the nature of addictions but there is always a catch. What happens when the highs get lower and you try to hold onto the feeling of happiness long after your emotions provide any joy? Like any addict, we wait for the next fix. Our assumption is that we are addicted to our desires and that they are reaching a dangerous zone.

Foods are our most dangerous wants because eating fuels nearly every other want. When you eat junk food, it tastes good at the time. About half an hour later you feel the after effects of your meal. Bloated you feel like sleeping it off. What tasted so good at the time wears off. That contributes to addiction as the food is full of fat, salt and sugar, when craving the same food again the next day.

When you overeat, you feel guilty. You know that there are healthier options yet you choose an unhealthy one. You feel guilty especially knowing that you have made a bad choice. You judge yourself as bad. No one goes into a fast food store thinking they are going to choose a healthy option. This is why you feel guilty. This guilt contributes to your addiction because you feel bad about yourself; which in turn leads to repeating the same behaviour. The guilt cycle starts all over again.

Lacking responsibility for your actions means you're too ready to blame others for your actions. Governments are the biggest culprits here. They are like overbearing parents saying that they will take care of all your problems, while stripping you of all control over your actions. Parliament thinks that you are unable to take care of yourself so strip us of all responsibility.

We can't see a way out of this state of desires. Governments, democracy, education, health and economics rob us of seeing a way out of this mess. All of these systems have grown large and bossy; the nanny state knows best. Instead of being a patient or voter or a student, we have instead this attitude of a nanny that knows what we need. They take care of our responsibilities while we take care of our desires by citing the mantra, greed is good.

When you are robbed of all accountability for your actions, you swim in inaction. Climate change won't be remedied by any individuals but by a collective cultural shift that takes a lead of making individuals do what's in the best interest of mother nature. A united group has the will to act in our best interests. Only community support for such action will save us from ourselves.

# Chapter 1: The end of desires

We are calling for moderation; the middle way between pleasure and pain, and not aestheticism. An example of the aesthete is any faith where monasticism is practiced. What we are against is the belief that aesthetes live in moderation. We don't view choosing to sleep on a mat, eating once a day and getting up at 4 am to meditate, as moderate.

Inaction will be a win for economic growth, greed and an increasing population. Maybe if we questioned this hegemony for a minute, we would find that is a good summary of what is wrong with human thought. Greed is opposed to moderation and rapid growth leads to ever increasing suffering.

The current economy isn't working and many in the US would agree. In 2008, the residential real estate market crashed with devastating effects. As we write this, the US stock market crashed to its third biggest one day drop in history. Do you still believe that greed is good now? There has to be another way, a more moderate way.

As we have seen economic growth is more volatile than most people think; especially rapid growth. Moderate growth is a better, more stable way; slow growth is more sustainable growth. At a time advertised as prosperous, 47% of Americans are living month by month. There is a mismatch between the American dream and the reality. We propose a moderate way out.

Voting with your dollar is a good start. By focusing on your spending; buying your needs rather your wants. This change in focus will reap large rewards in terms of the family budget. There will be a corresponding improvement in terms of savings for sustainable housing, transport and natural resources. The key to shifting demand from desires purchasing to required purchases is voting with your income rather than debt.

These days there is a tendency to owe, owe, owe. Remember that greed is fuelled by desires. The more wants that have, the more money that owe. Cutting our wants leads us to curb our spending and debt. We have to pay our debts first before we can enjoy not owing the banks.

Imagine a world that was debt free and stock market free. There would be lower highs and higher lows. The disparity between the rich and poor would narrow. A needs driven economy would enable the spread of necessities far into Africa. A needs driven sustainable will deliver all this and more.

Sustainability is the next focus; food and resources that are replenishable and those that aren't. A new environment with new industries who renew the environment will arise. Present technology fills landfills with old devices and cables that aren't recyclable.

To replace the mantra of greed is good, we need to come up with a new economy. A new economy is one that focuses on people's needs. The new economy is formed from voting founded on spending. If every family voted with their dollars in a needs driven economy, the world would be a better place. A new mantra focused on sharing and replenishable resources; a new economy that is better for our health and better for nature.

Whether we want to reduce population, democracy or education the same principle applies; vote with our dollars. The individual's desires have led to this precipice; the individual cannot be trusted to spend their dollars or vote wisely. Individual empowerment is another failed experiment in our history.

Spending our money wisely would make every oversized institution sit up and take notice. Every institution could be downsized through a decrease in demand. We don't advocate having these services undersupplied or under state control. We don't need a nanny state to govern services.

# The end of suffering

We look forward to an age where we no longer have cravings for personal desires. Our needs should rule over our desires. To achieve this, we need to change our thoughts about desires. We don't need to live a monastic or aesthetic life. Society has become obsessed about servicing desires. The servicing of needs for food, shelter and sanitary facilities once attained is labelled poverty; a poverty of desires.

Having an end of wants means an end of suffering; we need to practice the end of wanting. The only way we know to curb desires is to practice mindfulness. Mindfulness is decluttering your mind. Your mind is the main impediment to living a peaceful, calmer and insightful life. As soon as your mind is clear of thinking, you will be at peace.

The end of wanting must free you from defilements. Defilements are wrong views or ill will towards others, uncovered by your practice. This means focussing on one thing, the breath. The test of your spiritual practice is the way you treat others. You will find getting angry will be a test of your spirituality. To avoid unhelpful thinking, we should focus on practice.

To understand pain and suffering you need the right place to start to treat them effectively. Pain has causes; such as a hammer falling on your toes. We can't avoid pain; especially at birth and death. Suffering always follows pain around like a shadow. Most people when they hurt themselves they experience pain followed by suffering. The extent of the shadow depends on how we react to the pain afterwards. Those who experience fear, worry or anger in response to pain are likely to overreact and their pain will last longer.

We all experience pain during our lives. If you couldn't feel pain, your life would be fairly short. Everyone else has to feel pain; whether physical or mental. It is a part of life for all sentient beings.

Whether insects feel pain is a valid point. They flee when they are in danger. This suggests that they are aware of being in pain. What we do know about insects is that there couldn't be any life on earth; they co-evolved with plants.

Our fear of pain is largely due to our views of it. Instead of pain being thought of necessary, our tendency is to think of it as optional. We have become immune to most pain due the effectiveness of drugs. It isn't nice being in pain so drug manufacturers come up with solutions for every pain problem. That view causes us problems in our understanding of suffering. Painkillers don't weaken our suffering; in fact they boost our suffering.

Pain is natural. Isn't suffering a natural part of being in pain? You experience pain first but suffering is optional as it is a state of the mind. Most animals accept pain but we humans by denying our pain magnify it. Suffering as a mind object is a learned object; we learn that suffering follows pain. We observe our parents suffering so we suffer. There is no physical pain so why do we suffer? The irony is that we suffer through not allowing ourselves to feel pain; a desire not to be hurt.

What mental pain? Pain in this context means emotional anguish. There two natural reactions; flight or fight. These two are not emotions but we reinvent them into an array of emotions. We get angry when we are not in danger, so we fight; we are afraid of embarrassment so we flee. They were intended as survival mechanisms; we have perverted them into emotions. Emotions are dangerous things if we follow them.

It is necessary to see that they are two separate states; pain and suffering. Think after the initial pain there is no suffering; this shows that they can be separated. There is pain which is a physical reaction; then there is suffering, an emotional reaction; when one reduces the other reduces too. We are born and die in pain; this a necessary part of life. Suffering is the cause of emotional anger, anxiety and fear.

So we can treat suffering but not cure pain. Unfortunately most people don't know this because they don't practice mindfulness daily. Without mindfulness they don't realise the cause of suffering. Due to their separate natures suffering can be cured; the wise are those who are able to mitigate pain. The key is to be in a peaceful state and not to feel frightened; fear is the main ingredient of suffering.

Those who don't practice have to put up with some hurt during and after the pain has gone; due to pain being in an emotional mental state beforehand. Pain is here to stay: if you remove the mental anguish, then you are able to reduce it.

Let's look at a situation when we're either mad, worried or afraid. You don't register that your breath gets shorter. Anger grows as the breath gets shorter before you explode in a rush of swearing. Worry and fear lead you to shorten your breathing. That's one reason mindfulness focuses on your breath.

When we reduce our mental anguish, we can laugh at your impending death and your pain during life; that's one reason that they call laughter the best medicine. While laughing during pain only occurs for experienced practitioners, you can keep your respiration long by smiling; reducing the pain and suffering. Smiling is an unrated pain killer.

## Tourism

We all welcome a holiday. What about travelling overseas? It won't surprise you to learn that travel is a huge industry. You may not realise that vacations are a major cause of climate change. The air pollution of travelling by planes, trains and automobiles. Waste is caused by eating in a non-sustainable way and their waste products. Any travelling leads to poor air quality and the use of fossil fuels.

As more people holiday by seeing the world, tourism is a luxury that we cannot afford to continue given our soaring population. Tourism is a desire that we don't need. If the majority travelled internally rather than externally the world would be a cleaner place. We ignore the pollution while we enjoy the luxury.

There are technological solutions; such as virtual reality (VR). VR is more viable than you think. There numerous advantages: imagine not having to travel for 24 hours or more; imagine accessing the Louvre,

Mexico and Galapagos Islands from your lounge room; imagine avoiding the queues to popular destinations; and, many more.

The sustainable use of technology is our responsibility. Rather than using more natural resources, we need to be smarter about recycling and sustainability. The prediction is in 30 years humans will have over more than 10 billion mouths to feed.

## Chapter 2: Risking earth's health

We created a world of suffering and wants; we realise that our planet is sick and requires treatment. We also risk our own health; our own hell on earth. Where else could it be? Creating suffering is hellish. We will only have ourselves to blame.

Maybe we are creating the conditions for our own demise. Stripping nature bare in the pursuit of our desires seems foolish after the fact; maybe climate change will go too far for us to turn back and reverse the damage done. We are the author of our own suffering. Our habits are the cause of all anguish.

There is a choice: either cease wanting or you will suffer the consequences. The suffering is hidden because desires are extolled, sold and the price is good; through the economies of scale. This is a recipe for disaster. We avoid taking responsibility by making responsibility diffuse.

All we would need a few insects, some plant material and enough water, then life could bounce back. The practice of liberation from agony means we could find a way out; an enlightened species that knows the right way out of suffering.

The condition of the atmosphere being restored is going to take a long time; perhaps many millennia. The atmosphere was created when the earth was born. As the earth cooled volcanoes were formed that pumped the required gases for an atmosphere to be formed. Whether the intensity of present volcanoes could replicate similar greenhouse friendly gases is highly unlikely due it having counteracted all the greenhouse gases we produce.

By converting greenhouse gases into atmosphere creating ones, we may be able to buy extra time. By converting greenhouse gases into CO2 and other atmospheric friendly, we will have the required time to curb climate change. What if we added planting trees, including rescuing the Amazon forest? This would be a longer term term solution but it would help. Could we pump out enough greenhouse friendly gases?

## Sustainability

We would do well to adopt sustainability as a mantra until we treat desires. At least sustainability would provide a non-threatening way to gently introduce the reality that we are at fault of causing climate change. The benefits of living sustainably are many and we hope that this and STEM may be enough to the global temperature at the same levels. It is a good place to start.

We require accelerated change to bring us towards a working solution. Everything we eat should be sustainable, we need to have a renewable source of protein and a renewable source of fuel. We must phase out every use of fossil fuels.

How do you sell the sustainability message? Associate climate change with sustainability. When you think of one, you should automatically think of the other; by making a habit out of doing the right thing for the viability of life on this planet. Climate change is a real danger to our species but there is a way out; spend your money only on sustainable resources.

The companies involved in the stripping of natural resources know that the damage is being done and the potentially irreversible effects. They need to be persuaded that doing the right thing will pay off commercially. As always companies won't act in our best interests so we'll have to give them a financial disincentive to change; to compete with those businesses that model sustainability.

We are cutting down trees at an alarming rate. No greater example is clearing of the Amazon. The Amazon has been described by experts as the lungs of the planet. Through our attitude to the Amazon ignoring the environmental consequences, cutting down more than is sustainable. We already have trees that are grown sustainably; we don't need to harvest trees in the Amazon.

The absence of insects will only allow us to live on for 50 years. Extinctions are happening at an accelerating rate. This is a snowball effect where greater extinction of species follows. This applies earthwide; no one can escape the loss of insects.

What factors will tip us into action? Being in personal danger, recognising the link between our desires and climate change, and knowing that eventually there will be a point of no return. Climate Change (CC) requires a reverse tipping point.

The cleverest have gotten us into this mess, they aren't going to act unless there are financial incentives to do so. How are we to change this mindset that rapid economic growth is in the common good? We need to focus their attention on the downsides of recessions, consumers voting with their dollar to support sustainability and the instability of rapid growth.

Species have life cycles. Species follow the natural way of all things. Changes in temperature will be all species undoing. This doesn't have to be the end of humanity but a rebirth.

United we stand, divided we fall. We need all hands on deck to avoid this tragedy; endangering. We still work on our desires. What then? Treated all with loving kindness; like everyone as yourself.

At present, the presence of too many people are imbued with their self-image, wealth or fame and this is killing us. Their self love is a symptom of the strength of their desires.

## Actions not donations

Today wants have become a synonym for needs, as pain has become a synonym for suffering. Wants are mistaken as a synonym for needs because this a way to keep the status quo where everyone is represented has a vested interest. We need to separate needs from wants in our understanding. Because if we can't separate the two there may be devastating consequences.

To cure suffering, we need to separate pain and suffering. We can't treat them as having two separate causes. One is a mental state, suffering; the other is a physical state, pain. Once you treat them as separate conditions, you avoid mistaking them for the same thing.

Anguish doesn't respond to painkillers; anguish responds to the same treatment as desires. If mental anguish has an individual cause and it's not physical pain, then we will be able to view suffering as a mental condition.

We are human beings and we all suffer. You suffer because you don't know the cause of suffering; you don't because there is a cause there is a cure. Once you acknowledge the cause you can practice the cure..

Do babies feel pain when they are born? They feel pain but no mental anguish. How can they suffer when their mind hasn't formed yet? Their brain is fully developed yet they have no knowledge of suffering yet. Babies learn how to suffer, when they copy the rest of us. It is worthy to note that babies cry for their needs, they have no desires yet.

The main test of suffering comes at our death. We expect pain and this causes worry, fear or anger. The mind gets involved before pain begins. We worry about the pain involved in dying; we fear being unable to control our pain; we get angry because we tell ourselves, this is unfair. Why do we die? Medical treatment stills the body while robbing the mind of experiencing dying, and sharing that experience with our loved ones.

Sharing the experience of death will become more poignant with the possible death of most humans. This possibility arises once we reach 10 billion people all contributing to climate change. We all have a vested interest in the survival of the next generation or the misery of knowing we will all be affected. The uncertainty of the timeline is part of the problem. Those who put economic growth ahead of a changing climate versus those who want continued population growth to avoid the economy slowing.

We need to stop worrying about economic growth. What we can do is remove all road blocks. First priority is to remove all politicians. We need to vote directly on anything that is related to climate change. Our need to curb all desires is a priority. Our need for representation is over. What we need is direct democracy.

What do you know about direct democracy? In his Tedtalk, César Hidalgo explains direct democracy without mentioning the change in climate. He envisions a fully automated direct democracy in 30 years. We can't afford to wait that long because it's going to take decades after we take action to undo the damage. We need to take action to fix a broken democracy now.

Do we dislike politicians? We don't like how they run the country and we don't trust them to resolve climate issues. But there is a better way than the status quo and it's called direct democracy.

Let's start with the argument against taking a direct form of voting: cognitive dissonance and the move away from a universal voting system; both are interrelated. Cognitive overload would involve work against making your vote count because of the share number of bills before parliament. There would be too much to do daily or weekly to make a direct democracy viable. We also need to keep voters interested. 'I don't understand many of the bills and I don't have the time,' you say.

Direct democracy runs the risk of individuals using their vote for their desires. Direct voting may lead to a similar situation. If there are many gaining their desires instead of few, is this a bad thing? Maybe we are trying to fix a broken system. We need to move away from our wants; we need to break bad habits.

You need to lessen the cognitive load. Voting through groups is one option. We know that the crowd will be wiser than individuals. We have tried voting by democracy; why not invest power in the family or the community. We believe that the family has the knowledge, experience and life skills. The family or extended group covers these bases well. What we need most is for everyone to make a mental link between suffering and desires.

Who creates the bills? In direct democracy, the same people create the new bills, discuss new laws and vote whether they should be submitted to law or not. If these votes are decided by group decision making, research has been shown that groups make better decisions than individuals; if there is discussion and debate. This is an ongoing discussion on how to improve the system.

The second reason to argue against direct democracy is because it is against the status quo. Democracy is sacred; this is the best system on offer. 'I don't have the time for direct voting; far better to have a representative to vote for us'. We have spent centuries refining the system; why throw away the whole system. Any fix to democracy would have to fix a system from the ground up.

It is of grave concern that some of the wealthiest people get to vote on our behalf laws that represent their own wants. Despite checks and balances this is the current situation.

Voting by individuals is broken; legislation and the creation of laws is faulty. Most of us will welcome the redundancy of our politicians and their perks; many people will enjoy voting directly. They will enjoy the real power residing with the people; everybody having the opportunity to invest in a system that has real power. Our representatives are a roadblock. The time hasn't been wasted building a universal voting system, if it leads to a better one. There is a new way that relies on the wisdom of people.

We have a vested interest in voting directly without a politician. Voting on laws indirectly is slow; there is a long convoluted process involved. By voting directly, we would save time and money; a lot of money. We save on our representatives' pay, perks and travel. Not only do we get more engagement from a direct democracy, we can put to good work the funds saved our representatives and government assets.

We have discussed groups, families and communities as suggested voting groups. Our choice is to follow Malcom Gladwell ('The Tipping Point'). Gladwell estimates the group size where everyone is familiar with one another is 148. We rely on his research here. We suggest that the size of the group used for creating, debating and voting laws be around 150. This size group means that the cognitive load is spread and any discussion by a group will create meaningful votes.

# Chapter 3: Practice

The art of mindfulness is single-pointed in focusing on the breath. What do climate change and mindfulness have in common? Being calm helps us to make better decisions. Voting in a family encourages consensus making; weeding out bad decisions. Thinking about a view and talking about it are two separate ways to decide on various options. Our thoughts often fool us when they have no factual basis.

Being calm is more likely in a group. Angry and anxious views tend to level out under the group. The image of the angry mob isn't what we are talking about here. The angry mob hasn't vented to an audience of their peers. If calmness prevails in a direct democracy, who is there to get angry at? There are no representatives to get angry. This is one of the main benefits of direct voting; there will be more benefits than individual voting.

Where the practice becomes important is in the single-pointedness. We have personally experienced the joy that comes with the practice of calmness; this is known as calm-abiding meditation. It is the source for all other practice. When we know calmness, we are prepared for all other practices. Through repetition, we can attain calmness and forsake anxiety, fear and anger; freeing our minds for rational states.

We have found that focusing on the breath has prepared us for another stage of meditation. This practice is simpler than it sounds. Say that you have an argument with your brother. Then you pause and realise that you were partly to blame for the argument. So you do walking calm abiding meditation. When you have calmed down, you are able to say sorry to him.

By repeating his name on the outbreath, you are able to calm down and realise that by thinking bad thoughts about him created suffering for yourself. You love your brother as yourself; you are both human beings and you both suffer when you argue. With that knowledge you are ready to make peace between you.

Single-pointedness is common to all meditations. Whether you are sitting, walking or lying down there is the opportunity to meditate. When Ajahn Chah, a famous monk, was told by someone, 'Oh, I would love to do meditation but I don't have time' his reply was, 'Well, you have time to breathe don't you?' Few possessed the wisdom of the late Ajahn Chah.

If each group remains calm, then they will make better decisions. Most people claim that they don't have time to practice. Another wise monk said if everyone could meditate for 1 hour per day, then the world would be a better place. 'If you don't have time to meditate, then you need to do two hours.' Mindfulness will create a feedback loop. More mindful practice means you are calmer which in turn makes you want to practice more. More peacefulness makes it possible to attain bliss.

When focusing on your breath and bliss, other states are possible. Having insights allows you to make wiser decisions but being wise takes years of practice. When you have insights you're building up your wisdom one brick at time. Few people reach this level of practice perhaps one per two or more per generation.

Many Buddhists take the original Buddha as their teacher. Most will include a live teacher to lead them through the scriptures. The dharma the teaching can occur in many forms. 'God is in the scriptures.'. Whatever situation you find yourself in, there is an opportunity to learn.

You don't gain insights just by reading the scriptures; you have to practice before you make dharma. If you learn situations that arise in the present, then you have chosen the right teacher; who understands the dharma. My teacher says that, everything is dharma; you have the opportunity to learn from everything that you experience in the present.

Many of us need to practice mindfulness, if we are going to make even better decisions in our group. We have already heard that groups make better choices than individuals. With the right view we can make smarter decisions. The first right view is to practice. From there doing mindfulness will lead to insights of practical nature; a spiritual nature that leads to the revelation of all natures.

Direct democracy favours good choices. The insight to viewing others is that we all are the same; we are all human beings and we all suffer. Suffering is a great teacher; making mistakes. The practical insight is that we all share enough to recognise we are more similar than different. We all share 99.9% of the genetically similar genes to our neighbour. Our uniqueness drowns in the ocean of our sameness.

Why do we focus on differences, when there is no self according to the Buddha. You see one person you have seen us all. Not only are we genetically similar, we share suffering. Anguish is our destiny when we can't cure our desires. Wants arise when we act as individuals.

As more become sagacious so our collective spirit grows. If we had the highest form of being in our nature, then all the groups would be as one mind. We would still experience pain as this a natural state of living. As a collective, a unified group, there would be no need for individual direct voting as there would only be one vote.

## Responsible not rights

If going to climb out of this grand canyon we have dug ourselves, then we have to admit that we are responsible for this crisis. We need to admit our guilt. We all share the responsibility by focusing on fixing this situation.

Forty years ago in 1980 the world's population was 4.4 billion. We reached a threshold where the accumulated damage to the atmosphere was endangering the planet. Our move from the 'green' to the 'orange' zone slipped silently by our standard of living rose like never before. The planet wasn't totally clean since the Industrial Revolution but our population and pollution were a slow boiler in 1980.

Fast forward to the present and our having reached an orange danger zone. Due to our having an unsustainable population and number of wants. In 2050 will reach 10 billion people, we will reach a 'red zone' a tipping point where we have fewer option can reverse the damage done

Our selfish desire for continued rapid economic growth at an unsustainable level is due to fear. Because they are afraid of recessions; so afraid of the failure of the economy that they are trying to hang on to fast growth at all costs. What's wrong with steady growth? The highs may be less spectacular but so are the recessions.

Our generation has been responsible for the most damage in the last 40 years. It is only going to get worse through the economy growing, the population increasing. What can we do to help? A dairy and meat free diet with sustainable fish will help; vote with your shopping. After 5 billion people occupied the world we reached our first tipping point because our lives were no longer sustainable by the environment.

Our economy and wants have grown rapidly with the economy since 1980. A growing middle class meant there were people who could afford their wants. We believe the growth of the middle class is both a good and bad thing. It's good that the majority have everything they need. If we all lived sustainably having everything that we need and curbed our wants, then population would not be a factor in any tipping point.

We only have to curb companies' power to meet our goal of lowering the causes of our changes in our weather. Restrict the supply of our desires and increase the demand for our needs in a needs-only economy. Companies respond to demand. Demand has obvious causes and we call this dollar voting.

The world cow population has grown exponentially in the last 40 years because people like red meat and dairy even when there are sustainable options available. Developing countries own the most cattle. The number of cows is unsustainable. We have to change our wants for meat and dairy products.

The economy is run by emotions. Our desires play their role in the emotional rollercoaster ride that is our economy; emotions are in the driver's seat. There is no better place to witness this then the stock market.

What difference would it make to the world to take out every stock exchange? Companies couldn't grow as fast when the main source of capital fund raising is removed. Governments have called for all trading to cease, during the coronavirus. Companies are claiming that if the coronavirus stopped trading this would end in losses; this would only compound market anxiety. 'Circuit breakers' have halted trading three times in the last 100 years.

Public companies would have the most to lose. Private companies who built up their businesses the old fashioned way are the most secure.

We created the mantra that greed is good; we created the conditions in which some people get rich quick. Wealth created by investing in shares is a thing of the past; people being rich on paper will now face the recession. Let's not allow this speculation on our future to continue.

Your wanting to be rich is part of the root cause; your wanting to have a large house; a bigger car and the latest model. You desire wealth, beauty and fame. When you think like this you need to learn the law of impermanence. We want to hold onto everything without changing anything; this impossible because everything is subject to change.

Hopefully this will bring a new paradigm; one of not being focused on wealth and beauty; one that is based on compassion. Is this wishful thinking on our part. How can we cure bad habits, wrong views on what is important and the reinstatement of a values based society? With good old fashioned peer pressure.

Peer pressure disappeared a generation ago. Not teenage peer pressure but in adults. There are no neighbourhoods that left for adult pressure to conform to social norms. Now we follow the pressure of teens in this youth centered culture. In my youth, there was an intolerance of not conforming that led to kick up the bum. It was a moral based society that had consequences. We are not saying it was a perfect community but we showed respect for it's elders.

Respecting your elders is not an outdated practice but few conform to it now. It is a practice that has lasted thousands of years; now that it's gone what has left is a youth culture. Forty years ago our culture shifted, why? Because employees earned enough to become comfortable, overweight and lazy. Their wages have increased but this has had two bad effects; bad karma and a lack of calmness.

Bad and good karma is due to the way we treat others; not good or bad luck. Calmness is a still pond in which our peace of mind is reflected. This calmness has been replaced by a rapid river. This is a big problem because of our lack of respect. This situation was made worse by wants; a society fueled by desires.

The Coronavirus may give us a chance if a recession sets in. Why? Because if the middle class are jolted by large spending cuts then that means they can only afford the essentials. Will we learn a lesson from this? We hope so otherwise, we will regress to the status quo. That's a pity because it could have been so different.

Let's look at the economy. A focus on slow growth would have had less consequences; a focus on rapid growth has led us into a deep recession. Economics plays an invisible hand in climate change. It made us less spiritual, created more doubt and left people lost. There is a lack of direction that could be solved by direct democracy making a smaller economy.

Will direct democracy save us from a super-sized economy? All roads in direct voting lead to smaller companies focused on supplying our needs. The road block is big governments and their representatives. Take these politicians out of way and we have direct democracy; no sane person would want to go back to dictators, communism, sovereign monarchs or socialism. Direct democracy would take real power out of the few and give it to many; unlike the current version of democracy.

If individual voting continues, then the group will become irrelevant. The group doesn't belong to a class. When we see how the middle class arose, there doesn't seem to be a justification for investing a majority status on the basis of a definition of class.

The middle class arose out of economic fortune. Suddenly the average Jane could have luxury items that were previously reserved for the wealthy. Families with both parents working paying for their expanding lists of wants, an unhealthy lifestyle and no downtime leading to stress. The middle class were an accident of a fortunate growth in the economy enabling everyone's wishes. The middle class has grown to fill the gap in demand.

We thought that the middle class represented the middle path. The middle way is following the eightfold path and not aestheticism; it's an ethical journey. Following the eightfold path is not onerous. You just find values, like the right view, and discover what they are through the insights generated during meditation practice. Self-observance, self-restraint, and cultivating kindness and compassion take practice but they aren't so onerous that lay people can't attain them.

The middle class is a major source of suffering to themselves. The speed of the economy is among the causes of their suffering. The expanding global middle class, their appetite for all of their wants and the increase in population contribute to climate change.

Mass production of wants is based on demand yet these companies are responsible for the methods of production, specialisation that led to further economies of scale and feeding off the profits by sourcing out to developing countries with much lower wage rates.

Desires have been a feedback loop. The hitch for the advertisers of luxury products was the economy. Companies had to work hard for their sales but slowly at first this created a feedback loop where advertising planted desires in our minds. The satiation of the desires required more income and by 1980 families had enough disposable income to give their children gifts throughout the year.

Families squeezed into a newly made middle class. Since 1980 the middle class has expanded to outnumber both the rich and poor; in 1980 disposable income reached a tipping point where the middle class grew along with their expanding waistlines. In the intervening years, desires have flourished to the point where the majority can have their wants filled daily; if they wish. This is following the eightfold path; an ethical path. It has been fascinating to watch food going from a necessity to a desire.

We believe that food fuelled our desires. Our desires grew the more we ate unhealthy food. Our desire for food spawned a whole new industry; the diet industry. This led to the yo-yo dieting. We would start a little bit overweight soft around the middle. You can guess the rest; starting a diet or exercise regime; starting the new regime with vigour; failing to maintain unrealistic programs; slipping backwards; giving up and interpreting as failure; putting more weight than you started with; feeling low in self-esteem you turn to more food. Thus a new addiction to dieting and bingeing has become one of the large industries.

This food addiction is a major player in the overall scheme of desires; demand and supply. It displays the lack of personal, corporate and medical lack of responsibility by individuals who would claim they have a right to eat, drink and buy whatever they want. This is where financial disincentives can play a big influence on desires. Yes you have the right to what you want to eat but you have the responsibility to select food wisely; a lifestyle tax.

## Rights are individualistic

Rights are selfish without responsibility. Do we need rights? The obvious answer is yes. The unobvious is no. We don't need rights because they are built into our responsibilities. We have our rights and responsibilities the wrong way. We humans who lived previous millenia stated 'thou shall not..'

Do these responsibilities apply to human rights? Of course they do, you shouldn't have rights first; where do these rights come from, if not our accountability. These privileges don't last during times of turmoil; they are the first to disappear whenever society is in turmoil.

When times are tough accountability is required. Accountability is required because being responsible is what's required in this moment; rights are an argument we can't afford when faced with danger. Rights are a privilege whereas accountability for one's action is necessary for our survival. We are all responsible for this changing climate; we don't have the option to continue as if the earth doesn't matter.

Less people will mean less air pollution; less spending will mean less desires; if the economy goes into recession. This will give us time to change our bad habits. Our survival may be dependent on old habits to break the cycle that caused the global temperature to rise.

Unlike a social tipping point this a cumulative effect reaching a tipping point with multiple sufficient and necessary factors. If the $CO^2$ emissions continue to rise, then we will reach a tipping point irrespective of the other causes. Nature will be too slow to react to build up the atmosphere.

One rule is at least do no harm to the environment. If we had followed this rule the last 40 years, perhaps we wouldn't have found ourselves in such a mess. When we don't follow this rule, we have immoral actions due to harming nature.

Ethics is more to do with our actions and when we intentionally cause suffering to others, we suffer. Suffering provides an opportunity to learn, if we are willing to listen. Human nature is ethical with an amoral component.

Amorality is an action that fills our desires and gives no heed to whether it causes others to suffer. When the karmic effect is operating, we feel guilt when we have the intention to harm others. We all have a conscience that makes us feel bad when we do something wrong.

The only way we can see to help is to cure our desires. Creating sustainable options is a viable solution before taking the bigger step of repairing the environment. The damage done in the last forty years may not be reversible without technological intervention. There has been more damage done in the past forty years than in the previous four hundred. Science, Technology, Engineering and Math (STEM) may save us if we have the right intentions.

Bill Gates warned us of the danger of the next virus 5 years ago. Did we take the right approach as recommended by Bill? Of course not. Yes there is a threat to all life on this planet and we need to act now. These actions depend on whether we have the will to adopt direct democracy. Yes, direct democracy will aid our decisions. If we vote in a direct democracy that removes representatives, we will make better decisions. If we foster group decisions, then we will make great decisions.

One of the obstacles in achieving this is that direct democracy is a new idea which will require lots of information and the endorsement of scientists and companies. We'll make that time if we realise our children will suffer the consequences. People complain about politicians looking after number one but don't have the will to change. There is an alternative but we need to find a way to implement it.

What will it take to implement voting directly? Socialites know up to 150 people who believe what they say. Experts who people trust to give them the right information. Persuaders make changes happen through their persuasiveness. These three different personalities will hopefully aid the wisdom of the group.

Is there a relationship here in the rise in rights and factors that affect global warming? There is: the population rose dramatically; the amount of carbon dioxide rose; methane levels increased in the atmosphere; oxygen levels decreased; air pollution and waste products in the environment increased dramatically; carbon monoxide levels continued to increase; etcetera. Any population increase will increase the number of individual rights.

# Chapter 4: Less is more

The less we pollute earth the more we will benefit from what nature has to offer. Forests will be revived; air quality will rise, even in the largest cities; plastic bottles won't be washed up on the beaches of the world; species won't be going extinct at 10x their normal rate; those species who are struggling will thrive; all food could be organic; and, much more benefits.

Three or more populations need to be lowered. Cows, sheep and humans. Cows are among the greatest greenhouse gases produced with their methane. We could reduce the cow population easily by half with bulls siring less cows. Same thing with sheep. Financial incentives could be in place to make it viable to change cattle stations into crop based farms.

The human population is the most problematic because it involves us and economic growth depends on the number of people; due to increased demand. Perhaps a picture of the panic and speculators who hoped to profit when supplies became short, spent on stocking up every non-sustainable item, especially toilet paper.

I saw a talk by Tshering Tobgay, on the Third Pole melting which would lead to catastrophic effects on Asia. Downstream floods would break dams in its way. This is all due to the current increase of melting of the Third Pole. According to the 2019 Global Change Report, the annual rise in temperature was 1.15 degrees centigrade above the pre-industrial average; Tshering claimed that the report with its recommended limit of 2 degrees would allow the accelerating melting to continue.

Perhaps the least considered effect of climate change is that insects may be going to be extinct in fifty years; if the same rate of extinctions occur. That is a major concern as this would signal the end of all species on earth. If temperature doesn't reduce, all insects may die. If all of the insects die, we will face starvation.

Why are we suddenly focusing on insects? Because the decreasing number and species of insects should be a priority given 50 years. Why should we care about insects, when there are higher priorities? Insects are the foundation of all life; all living beings depend on the existence of insects. If life disappears due to our ignorance of the consequences of our desires, then this will be a tragedy of our own making.

Less air pollution would help slow the temperature increases but temperature decreases are more difficult to achieve. Lowering temperatures would take at least 2x the amount of time it took to raise them. How do we start to lower the temperature? We're hoping that climate scientists will have the answer and that we'll work it out with the help of STEM. There are an estimated 30,000 species left of insects; down from approximately 3 million forty years ago.

What happened in 1980 that makes it a watershed year? The temperature began rising and didn't stop; it is still rising today. Prior to 1980 there had been increases and decreases but they were in equilibrium; there were rises and falls but not one dominating. We are not talking about a gradual change, we are talking about a temperature that the earth has not seen in modern history.

The priorities are lowering the global temperature, reversing the extinction of insects and improving the air quality. None of these measures will work if we don't get to the heart of what is causing the suffering of insect extinction. Abstinence is a required, if we want to live past this century. It's a necessary condition as are reversing the extinctions of insects.

We suggest a multi-faceted approach to reverse climate change; we have to reduce populations, waste, and should increase air quality and the conservation of endangered species. The most important to conserve is the population of insects.

Will these measures be enough to reverse the damage? If our population stays at 7.5 billion and then starts to drop, we have the opportunity to reverse the number of wants. Even at 7.5 billion people that is a lot of wants to cure. If everyone adopted a sustainable lifestyle this would help.

## Less greenhouse gases

We need to reduce the use of utilities. Not because they are not necessary but because we produce them unsustainably. The use of natural resources that are not sustainable especially as the human population grows. We have to convince developing countries especially China and India to reduce their population growth below 1.9 children per couple. This is going to be a hard task especially when we have an incentive for population growth; economic growth.

There is a feedback loop; the greater our wants the more we need to grow our market share. The greater our wants for offshore manufacturing and information technology the greater global growth. The only reason that we went offshore is because their wage rates are so low. We don't care that the average person has to work two jobs to make ends meet.

Paying developing nations fair wages is bad for our economy. Do we really need to bring in-house all manufacturing and technology; manufacturing yes. What about technology? This a more difficult question, do we have the prerequisite knowledge?

Technology requires local manufacture of all devices. Is technology durable and disposable? Not yet but there is an incentive to take the lead. You only have to talk to friends looking for ways to get rid of old devices.

One dispute that could erupt is over cattle. Countries that rely heavily on meat production will baulk at the suggestion that they reduce their cattle production. Brazil, China and the US as the largest three, must take the lead in reducing. We predict that they will refuse and probably cite the reason for sovereignty. So we need to unite to place large tariffs on their meat products as a deterrent. Financial disincentives do work; it's just a matter of making local products cheaper.

Meanwhile agriculture could serve to save the earth from our avaricious nature. We could place an emphasis on growing local fruit and vegetables. Here a radical idea that is overdue: make all fruit and vegetables free. The poor wouldn't have to go hungry and they would become healthier. The saving in medical bills could pay for the free vegetables by itself.

Transport is a huge source of greenhouse gases and natural resources. Whether we use trains, planes and automobiles to supply goods, provide us with a holiday or to drive the kids to school. Do we really need so much transport? Do we need overseas holidays? Do we need private cars? Do we have unsustainable modes of transport? We must get used to living sustainably. There are opportunity costs to saving ourselves; that we can't deny.

Millions of people have been working from home. Maybe that's a good thing given teleconferencing and other technology. Technology enables most to work from home. What if driving licence was a privilege and not a right based on age? There may be a significant improvement in air quality; especially big cities. The challenge is to get air quality up and global temperature down.

## Less wants

There is something that we all share - suffering. When we want something that we don't need, we suffer. From the chinese factory worker who has to work multiple jobs just to make ends meet; to ourselves. We know that the reason behind shifting work overseas is wrong; we know that self-justifications like they provide jobs for developing countries may fool others but not yourself; hence you suffer.

There are eight cures for suffering. The Noble Eightfold Path is a moral practice and a way out of suffering. The most important ones are right view and wrong view; this isn't the selfish view that I am right and everybody else is wrong. Right view is built up by practicing mindfulness. Our ethics become brighter the more we practice, and the more we practice the brighter our values become.

It is a hard proposition to convince people that they cause their own suffering of the mind. That is the aim of this book but it is difficult to convince anyone who doesn't do the practice; suffering is always something out there. We enjoy the negative implications of, 'thank god that is not happening to me.' The truth is we suffer from anxiety; the world is a dangerous place and we can't trust strangers. It is a short jump to, you can't trust anyone.

If we acted as a country on the urgency of reversing climate change, we could act as persuaders. The same approach could be taken avoiding politicians; they have too much high maintenance. We need to remind citizens of their responsibilities and risks of their not acting.

Maybe we can persuade the current generation and the next generation? We have to act on the reversing of increases in global warming; a population drop in humans and cow/ sheep/ chicken; aim for zero air pollution and waste in 10 years; the use of natural resources as fuel to nil; going on holiday; and sustainable solutions for all. There are many things that we need to give up.

How are we going to implement direct democracy? Doubters will say, there's too little time to make such large political changes. This may take 10 years to implement both the changes necessary to lower global warming and take power away from the power of the representatives.

We don't believe that it will be hard to change voting. From what we have seen the catch phrase, every vote counts, has worn thin after decades of use. We believe that the majority are dissatisfied with the current system and haven't heard of direct democracy before. We feel change in the air and with these changes the turnaround on bills will be shorter. This may stop politicians from claiming, 'this is the best system that we have to work with.'

When we grow sufficient momentum, then we will be able to have an opting out of the political system at that stage. Do we have to win a general election to enforce the changes that we need to make or can we work within the current political system. We know that is the option that the current political parties and democracy would prefer.

If we have the will, then we'll look at countries like Switzerland which have a semi-direct democratic system. It will be a steep learning curve. For millennia the wisdom of the group was held by the elders. The modern equivalent would include women and minorities. There should be a role for wisdom.

Individual enlightenment plays no part in the wisdom of the group; it is life experience that counts. The wise provides a subgroup that has opted out of inclusion; for those who are unwilling or are unable to participate. Such an experienced committee should be mainly composed of retired or those retired due to health issues; anyone who can make a contribution.

Re-establishing respect for these elders who have a lot of experience should be a priority. The wisdom of the group makes any decisions of the collective wisdom. Democracy relies on a collection of individual votes and these aren't wise but popular needs and wants. Politicians who merely follow the party line irrespective of what their conscience tells them, suffer.

Due to our representatives and the media interest in the economy, we focus on it. Who owns the media? The wealthiest of the wealthy are those who own most of the media. That is why if you want to be Prime Minister, you need to be rich and they are going to vote based on economic factors.

A rapidly growing economy is preferred by most. The economy runs the whole of government now; it is in the driver's seat. What about the billions governments spend on health and education? Spending is great for the economy. Which came first spending or greed? They both co-evolved; when spending goes up greed goes up.

When spending goes down, greed bottoms out. Debt is great for the economy. In the end the bubble bursts, as it must, and everything comes crashing down. All for what? To supply the wants of all.

Now poverty is not a common good either and isn't what we mean by the middle way. The middle way is the path between desires and aestheticism; it is a mental state. The middle class had the perfect opportunity to find a state between where ethics and needs matter. Instead the middle class squandered the opportunity to be the first social group that places their needs before wants; greed prevailed.

Human nature is programmed by us to satiate our desires when our needs are met. When we were struggling to feed ourselves, our desires played a spiritual part in our lives to steer us away from our sins; our wants planned a path to the afterlife. The 20th and 21st centuries have built a middle class out of their prosperity; as result of increased wealth, we have generated larger desires. These desires reached a tipping point in 1980.

The income, spending power and the power of the new economy meant that 1980 was a pivotal date in the progress of climate change. In 1980 we had reached a tipping point in greenhouse gases that caused the global temperature to rise for the past 40 years. The tipping points we now face are the extinction of insects, climate change entering an irreversible danger zone and spiraling population.

Is the middle class to blame? Not really; the bulk of any blame has to come back to our base instincts. Whenever there is greed this presents an opportunity for wrong view but we can overcome our base desires. How do we know this is the wrong view? Through the practice of meditation; meditation is a path to wisdom.

It is important to know that physical pain normally precedes suffering; like hitting your thumb with a hammer. The exception to that is where the pain originates in the mind. But if we remove the mind's role in the process then we remove the cause of suffering; the wish not to be in pain. Then the endorphins can act in their role of reducing the pain.

# Chapter 5: Impermanence

Small changes are the norm. Think of your life; make you recognise each day there will changes that will lead you to age. Thinking of death makes you prepared for the end and makes your life more meaningful. Life isn't about being rich and famous; it is about how you treat others. If you treat others well, they in turn will like you and you will like yourself. This is what is meant by karma and leading a spiritual life.

A spiritual life and its practice is all you need to become wise; it's the foundation of all practice. We aren't born into this world alone. In the last two centuries, we have taken others for granted: our parents, friends, grandparents and other relatives; our tribe. The world is shrinking through self-isolation. Self-isolation is the way things are headed when they are past the current pandemic.

We have all heard of building up to something slowly using small manageable steps. This is the key to making changes in a sustainable way; by making small steps through building the foundations first. These we call incremental changes. If we add these up over a year, they will make a large change.

Progress in your spiritual practice will happen slowly. You might find you are going backwards sometimes. If you just stick to your daily practice, then you will make progress guaranteed. Why are we discussing personal progress? Because of the emotional decision making of the individual who doesn't practice. There is wisdom in a group that makes rational decisions rather than a personal.

Slow progress is good for growth and stable over time. One scientist says that the tracking of butterflies wouldn't be possible without citizen scientists; these insects co-evolve the first plants. Anything that brings scientists and citizens together is of benefit to everyone. We believe this approach may be too slow to have a major impact; it avoids the root cause of climate change.

Mathematics has a big part to play in greed. People assume that math is a tool manipulated by us; in fact equations are calculated out of desires. The problem with math in charge is that ethics aren't an integral part of math. You can tweak the numbers any way you want and this won't produce one ethic. Numbers solves number problems not ethical ones

There are rules of living that include sustainability. Healthy living concerning diets, exercise and avoiding stress have been built through thousands of years of accrued knowledge. This is especially true of medicine. Medicine traditionally relied on the wisdom of the elders. Medical treatment was brutal compared until the modern era was to treatment to dull the pain; as medicine was taken over by science. Previous forms were patient centered and were patient centered.

Small changes in medicine made a big difference over thousands of years. Similarly practical changes may take longer but lead to a great leap forward over time. Progress is good when it takes time. We live in a time where speed is associated as being a good thing. The faster you get a product to market; that you test a vaccine; manufacture a new technology. Speed is an economic good; you just have to treat slow growth with a heavy dose of sedatives.

Small changes are better because they require smaller steps. A needs based economy benefits from slow growth. The economy has to change so it might as well be for the better. Change is the one constant; people, matter and galaxies all change; birth, living and dying means that we all undergo the circle of life.

## Exclude politicians

What a tragic waste of resources our politicians have been. Parliament served the rich and always has done so, 'in the national interest'. That was okay when the parliament had less power and resources. Apart from starting wars, the next worst thing they have done is enabling desires as buying votes.

Creating GST and not taking away PAYE; going into debt based upon the assumption that borrowing to pay for health and education is good. Pondering why borrowing doesn't magically make better institutions the more cash is thrown at them. Parliament has neglected its responsibilities; the larger the government institutions have become the worse their performance has become.

Health cost is only one way to measure the performance of a hospital. If hospitals weren't just bottom of the cliff operations, then they could treat causes and not symptoms. The principle cause of treating patients today is their desire for food; predominantly unhealthy foods. Hospitals should be in the business of treating the whole patient.

In a needs based economy, this would go hand in hand with treating causes and not symptoms. Imagine the tradeoffs between the costs and savings based on the number of patients treated for all causes in specialist centres.

We have our values all wrong. Instead of compassion, we have mistrust rather than treat others with loving kindness, we feel resentment to others. Instead of using karma, we treat others based on the mood that we are in. Karma is a test of our spiritual nature. We should treat others equally no matter what mood we are in.

We have the wrong view on rights and responsibilities. It's also true that modern society reveres the young and the beautiful. What people don't realise is that everything changes. The young become old and no longer revered. We have donkeys before the cart. The elders should teach us with all their life experience. We shouldn't have the inexperienced leading the experienced.

There is a loss of values. When you have fashionable values not permanent values, they are desires. It's like one trying to hold onto beauty and wealth; impermanence intervenes and brings the valueless person down with a crash. When you are without values, then you are in a sea of doubt. You may be able to fool others that your values and goals are separate but you know for yourself.

A needs based economy needs a parity of price. A price parity means sustainable choices are the same price as unsustainable choices. This is usually achieved by raising taxes on unsustainable goods until they reach a tipping point; where through economies of scale healthy choices tip over due being equivalent. If you produce unsustainable goods, then you are going to be penalised to make way for a sustainable world.

Foods are a great example of everyday desires and could be a category that could be easily corrected, if we make it financially attractive to choose healthy options. All those living in poverty are a social group who eat unhealthily food due to it being cheaper now.

## Politicians' role change

Re-constitution of government may constitute voting: direct or semi-direct. Once we agree on the constitution, we can move onto enacting that system of government. We think that voting on a new system of government will excite people and will raise voter participation.

Individual direct voting will be most familiar to voters. This will be an improvement on our current system which has become too large to suit its original purpose. Our system of government has become outmoded. Direct voting without representatives is the best option.

"It may take months or even years for a bill to pass through Parliament. However, an urgent bill can be passed in a matter of hours or days. Well over 100 bills are introduced into Parliament each year and about 90 per cent of government bills are passed into law." (source https://peo.gov.au/). Where is the cognitive overload? Urgents bills can pass in a day. Why can't all bills be passed in a month in 12 votes per year?

Where is the need for representation? The bulk of the waste in taxes goes to these representatives, these politicians. Politicians are a major reason that PAYE wasn't abolished when GST was introduced. Everybody enjoys spending other peoples' money and this is true of the politicians. Rather than protests there was apathy. This worked in the politicians favour.

Then economics judged that debt was a good thing. This gave unlimited spending power to our representatives. When we borrow do we examine who is lending us money? Borrowing has a price; both sovereignty and the payment of interest. Serving $1 trillion dollars of loans in 2022-3 will cost us up to $25 billion in interest, when interest rates rise again. That's an average $400 per adult and child.

Time and time again we hear, 'this is the system we are stuck with'. It's broken and it doesn't need replacing? Our collective imagination is lacking, if we can't come up with a better system. Fortunately there is a better option on offer. How is direct democracy better? Direct democracy is like a fat free diet; it removes excess fat in our government.

Removing our representatives is the only forward. This move will replace debt and overspending with repaying debt and underspending. Replacing our representatives will enable direct voting which will mean that laws regarding changes of climate will be voted through quickly.

Voting directly will have numerous benefits: a fall in the interest in the economy; a voting system that will eventually replace the economy; democracy and capitalism are broken. This is due to them both working for the benefit of the extremely wealthy. Other interests include those of our representatives; taxes based on what you earn; not investing in sustainability. Voting for political parties and representatives will become a relic from the past; voting directly for bills becomes the norm.

Voting directly for bills will make every vote count. Think how disillusioned everyone is today with the current system. Up to 1.5 million of eligible voters did not vote in a compulsory voting system in 2019. We don't know the number who handed in a void voting sheet. The sheer number of candidates makes direct voting look simple by comparison.

9 781716 873461